MW00527266

Put Your House in Order

by Debbie Williams
of www.OrganizedTimes.com

We hope the information featured on these pages is helpful in your home and business organizing. What we say may not apply to your particular situation, or be totally current at any given time. Let's Get it Together© disclaims all warranties with regard to any information found anywhere in this study course, quoted from Let's Get it Together©, or sent from Let's Get it Together©, including all implied warranties of merchantability and fitness for a particular purpose. Let's Get it Together© shall not be liable for any indirect, special, or consequential damages, or any damages arising out of or in connection with the use or performance of this information.

Cover art and clipart from Microsoft Corporation's Online Clip Art Gallery.

TABLE OF CONTENTS

An Introduction 3

Chapter One: Get it Together! 5
    Step 1: Plan for Success
    Step 2: Sort through the Clutter
    Step 3: Organize Your Stuff

Chapter Two: Clutter Therapy for Your Home 25
    Step 4: Maintain Your System Daily
    Daydreaming Exercise

Chapter Three: It's About Time 42
    5 Steps to Becoming an Effective Home
    Manager
    How Do You Waste Your Time

Chapter Four: Purging Paper Clutter 77
    Closing Thoughts
    How to Contact Us

Chapter Five: Resources 94
    Websites
    Catalogs
    Books
    Recommended Products
    Organizing Labels

An Introduction

Are you a Christian parent? Do you feel the stress of wearing many different hats: chef, nurse, and even teacher? Then this course was written for you!

We have some things in common, my friend. I, too, am a busy parent. However, God has blessed me with parents who introduced me to the principles of time management and clutter control. They encouraged me to find additional resources at work and home that would help to keep me organized. When I first became a mother a few years ago, I assumed that every parent knew how to effectively manage her time, conquer clutter, and fight the chaos creators in her busy life. Was I ever wrong!

My mission is to share the tips and techniques that I have learned and adapted throughout the years with you – the busy parent. I want to help you become the very best that you can be. Let me take you by the hand, one baby step at a time, to walk you through the organizing process. Allow me to be your coach, giving you play-by-play instructions to help you learn new ways to manage your time, and *unlearn* the old habits that have kept you from being your best self.

When you choose to diligently pursue an organized life, then this study course will help you get your home, office, car, kids— your entire life in order. It's self-paced, which means you can pick it up and put it down again and again as you have time.

I know you will have many interruptions—that's what makes life so interesting; working at your own pace allows *for* rather than fights *against* them. The worksheets, action plans, and exercises (or HOMEwork) will provide the reinforcement you need to learn new habits. Some things will work, while others will not - it's entirely up to you to decide what you need in order to get yourself organized. And I'll be here, maybe not in body but definitely in spirit, to help you every step of the way.

Now let's get it together!

Chapter One: Let's Get It Together!

Daydreaming Exercise: Juggling Act

Picture a woman juggling small balls in the air, each labeled with the single words:
Self, Family, Career, and Spouse.

Each of the balls is the same size, made from durable materials that will bounce but not break if dropped or neglected. The ball labeled *Family*, however, is constructed from delicate crystal, a precious material that will shatter if not handled with care.

How do you think the woman will handle the FAMILY ball? Will she let it drop, only to shatter into a million pieces, never to be repaired? Or will she make sure she does everything humanly possible to keep that ball aloft, safe from harm?

My point in using this illustration is that a parent can juggle all the aspects of her life –career, self-improvement, and homemaking - but must continue to care for and protect the most valuable aspect of all: her family.

Make sure you are juggling the right priorities in your life, and continuing to care for the most prized of all: those that you love. Hold them dear and keep them aloft, even at the cost of other areas of your life—they're one of a kind and cannot be replaced.

HOMEwork –The Capable Wife

Read Proverbs 31:10-31, keeping in mind that the ideal woman described by King Lemuel (otherwise known as King Solomon) is a composite rather than a real person. Rather than being defeated by an ideal you can't possibly live up to, try instead to be inspired to be your very best. Use this as your motivation to be all you can be, for your husband, your children, yourself, and your God.

> *An excellent wife, who can find?*
> *For her worth is far above jewels,*
>
> *The heart of her husband trusts in her,*
> *And he will have no lack of gain.*
> *She does him good and not evil*
> *All the days of her life.*
>
> *She looks for wool and flax,*
> *And works with her hands in delight.*
>
> *She is like merchant ships;*
> *She brings her food from afar.*
>
> *She rises also while it is still night,*
> *And gives food to her household,*

And portions to her maidens.

She considers a field and buys it;
From her earnings she plants a vineyard.

She girds herself with strength,
And makes her arms strong.

She senses that her gain is good;
Her lamp does not go out at night.

She stretches out her hands to the distaff,
And her hands grasp the spindle.

She extends her hand to the poor;
And she stretches out her hands to the needy.

She is not afraid of the snow for her household,
For all her household are clothed with scarlet.

She makes coverings for herself;
Her clothing is fine linen and purple.

Her husband is known in the gates,
When he sits among the elders of the land.

She makes linen garments and sells them,
And supplies belts to the tradesmen.

Strength and dignity are her clothing,
And she smiles at the future.

She opens her mouth in wisdom,
And the teaching of kindness is on her tongue.

She looks well to the ways of her household,
And does not eat the bread of idleness.

Her children rise up and bless her;
Her husband also, and he praises her saying:

"Many daughters have done nobly,
But you excel them all."

Charm is deceitful and
Beauty is vain,
But a woman who fears
The Lord, she shall be praised.

Give her the product of her hands,
And let her works praise her in the gates.

What a powerful passage this is! Each time I read these verses, I can see many practical applications for the woman of today:

She has the **trust** of her husband (he relies on her sound judgment and wisdom in managing their household and guiding their children at home and in the community).

She **supports** her husband rather than badmouthing him to friends, neighbors, and her mother. This is the total opposite of what we often read on discussion boards, in women's magazines, or even hear discussed at our monthly BUNCO games.

She **clothes** her family in quality garments, which doesn't necessarily mean you have to become a professional seamstress to make your husband and your kids look well groomed. Hunting for bargains in the mall, shopping at resale shops, and finding treasure at rummage sales are all productive ways to find quality clothing at frugal prices.

She **produces** a variety of foods at her table, whether gourmet or down-home cooking. Healthy choices with fresh flavors are key to keeping her family eating well. She may not grow the fruits and vegetables, but she sure can pick out seasonal favorites to keep even the pickiest of eaters well fed.

She **rises** early to give her family a good day's start, rather than sleeping in and letting them fend for themselves. Getting up at the crack of dawn may not be in order for all of us, but setting your alarm to wake 15 minutes earlier than your husband and kids may give you just the time you need to jumpstart breakfast and school/work preparations.

She **works** productively in her home, whether as a homemaker or work-from-home mom. This is a woman who is a good steward of her time as well as her resources, making the most of what she has.

She **serves** the poor and the needy. Having a servant's heart doesn't just reflect how you make your offering each Sunday morning. This also includes donating goods and your time to the homeless shelter, vacuuming for the new mother down the street, or ministering to the friend whose husband just lost his job.

She is **prepared** for the winter months as well as the uncertain future. The pantry and freezer are well stocked, a disaster kit is organized and kept up to date with emergency items, and you're ready for the next season's change of clothing for your children and husband's needs. You live like a retail buyer, shopping a season ahead for seasonal clothes, linens, and foods that are fresh.

She is **wise** and teaches others the lessons she has learned, sharing her talents with those in her family as well as other women. But as wives and mothers we shouldn't just teach homemaking skills to others; we should be sharing all the positive lessons that we have learned in our daily walk with the Lord: how to have a servant's heart, how to start our day with the Lord, and how to be good stewards of our time and money.

She is **energetic,** not just doing busywork (see
Martha in Luke 11:38-42:

> *"Now as they were traveling along, He entered
> a certain village; and a woman named Martha
> welcomed Him into her home.*
>
> *And she had a sister called Mary, who moreover
> was listening to the Lord's word, seated at His
> feet.*
>
> *But Martha was distracted with all her
> preparations; and she came up to Him, and said,
> 'Lord, do You not care that my sister has left me
> to do all the serving alone? Then tell her to help
> me.'*
>
> *But the Lord answered and said to her, 'Martha,
> Martha, you are worried and bothered about so
> many things;*
>
> *But only a few things are necessary, really only
> one, for Mary has chosen the good part, which
> shall not be taken away from her.'*

She is **respected** by her husband and children,
praised publicly. Having the respect of our family
is a wonderful testimony to our job as wife and
mother. Wouldn't it be wonderful to overhear a
compliment from your teenage daughter rather
than hearing her bash you every chance she gets?

She is **godly**. Rather than worrying about what we look like on the outside or who we're seen with (vanity), we should fear the Lord, and let our works speak for themselves. This is being a beautiful woman of God.

HOMEwork –

• **Turn Down the Volume**

Turn down the radio or television volume in your home a click or two, and watch how quickly it affects the noise level and activities in your household.

If you don't see an immediate change, try this exercise a total of 3 times this week, and make a note of the changes it creates among your family members. You'll be amazed how easy it is to control the tone in your household.

• **Music Soothes the Savage Beast**
When frustration levels reach a peak – either for you, your spouse, or your children – try playing soft instrumental music in the background. Watch the results as children and teens begin to play quiet games, read, or take a nap, thereby lowering *your* stress level.

This is an excellent way to transition from busy activities (indoor wrestling, returning from play in the park) to quiet ones. It also works wonders during those times when your little one has outgrown naps but you both still have a need for some quiet time.

The 4-Step Process to Becoming an AWESOME Organizer

Getting organized is as simple as 1, 2, 3, 4! In my experience with coaching clients of all ages and backgrounds, from full time mothers to teenagers, this simple 4-step process works wonders in creating a manageable organizing system.

- Always begin with a plan.
- Sort through your clutter.
- Organize your stuff.
- Maintain your system on a daily basis

Step 1: Begin With a Plan

Lights, Camera, Action! – Before you plunge in over your head with your organizing project, you need to create an **action plan**.

Whether you use an **action plan** form such as those in this study course, a notebook, or a journal, it's important to start with a place to make notes and track your progress. It doesn't have to be fancy. Just make it user friendly and keep it on stand-by to refer to time and again.

Proverbs 16:3 says:

> *Commit your works to the Lord,*
> *And your plans will be established.*
> *(New American Standard)*

Now that's quite a promise, isn't it? Your organizational efforts will pay off big time because you have the strongest ally in the universe on your side. Remember to claim God's promise in Proverbs 16:3 each time you are feeling that you have the most disorganized house on your block.

Daydreaming Exercise: Seeing the True Scope of Things

Use a toy telescope or empty paper towel tube to get a realistic view of your clutter. This is one time it's okay *not* to look at the big picture. Zoom in on *one* area of your most cluttered space, and begin your organizational journey there.

Whether it's your kitchen countertop, the playroom, or your teenager's closet, focus on one little corner and then picture how you would *like* for it to look.

HOMEwork – Turning Nightmares into Dreams

- List your biggest **organizational nightmare** below, focusing only on one area for now.

  Organizational nightmare:

  _____

  _____

- Grab your action plan and write down the biggest **organizational day dream** you have for your newly organized space:

  #1 Day Dream:

  _____

  _____

  Are you ready to sort through the clutter now? Hang on—we're almost ready! But the planning step in your organizing homework is the most important step of all — remember all those swing sets and bicycles you tried to assemble *before* reading the instructions? Things didn't quite come together the way you wanted them to, did they? Bear with me as we create one last part of your action plan — then you'll be able to grab those totes and containers and fill them up again. And I promise it'll be worth the wait!

- It's time for action! Create an **action plan for success** sheet by listing all the rooms in your home on a large sheet of paper. Choose the one you would like to begin with and put the number "1" beside it. Find the second biggest organizing challenge and place a "2" beside it. Continue this prioritizing process until you have assigned a number to each room that you have selected.

  Set a realistic due date to organize your room and mark that date on your planning sheet. Don't just guess — grab a calendar and make a concerted effort to really reach your deadline. Mark each room as it is completed and include that date in your notes. This will serve as a realistic guideline for future projects, and will also remind that you *can* do this - and indeed you have)!

Step 2: Sort Through the Clutter

Now that you've created a plan for action, it's time to start sorting. Tackle one area at a time — and don't worry, the rest of the clutter will still be there when you're ready to conquer it!

HOMEwork -

- Create sorting labels by writing these words on 8.5 x 11 inch paper: TRASH, KEEP, SELL, UNDECIDED. Set up sturdy and easy-to-use sorting boxes for your organizing project. You might want to use cardboard boxes found at your local grocer's, or invest in banker's boxes (found at office supply stores) that can be reused time and again. (It's not the *packaging* that matters here, but the *process*.) Stick the labels onto your boxes. Use rubber cement or tape so that you can easily remove the labels to reuse them for another time.

- Begin by sorting the items in your cluttered little corner of the world. Tackle items one piece at a time, working around the room in a methodical fashion. You can go in a clockwise, counterclockwise or zigzag pattern — whatever feels most natural to you. Sort first, and then worry about the storage. Be sure to have plenty of those large empty boxes labeled: TRASH, KEEP, SELL and UNDECIDED. Remember not to get too attached to anything you touch during this step. Later, during your break, you can take the time to travel down memory lane while flipping through Junior's baby book, but right now it's time for action!

This is one of my personal favorites of the four organizing steps, because it's a no-brainer. Anyone can sort socks, shoes, shirts, papers, catalogs and so forth, putting like things together and tossing them into the appropriate boxes.

Get the kids to help you or invite a friend to join in. Listen to upbeat music to keep you moving and on track. Don't leave your sorting area to put things away, because you'll inevitably get sidetracked down the hall or in the laundry room, never returning to where you first began. Resist the temptation to stray, and stay on course!

Before you can take the next step in organizing (ORGANIZE), you must do something with all those objects you've sorted. Let's start with the easiest, and then work our way up to the more difficult (another effective time management tip).

- Take the "trash" box outside to your garbage can, dumpster or curb for pickup. Remove it from the room so that you don't have to deal with it taking up valuable space. That was easy, wasn't it?

- Now it's time to move on to the "sell" box. Carry it to your car or van to drop off tomorrow at your local resell shop. (Or delegate this job to a spouse or teenager who keeps getting underfoot.)

Let's take another look at that "undecided" box. When you've gotten this far in the process, it's much easier to be brutal, tossing things you would normally treasure. If anything is left in the box, move it to the hallway for now. You can tackle it after your upcoming break. (See? This won't be so stressful. We're only on Step 2 and you're already getting a break!)

That leaves you with the "keep" box, which is the only box of stuff you will actually be organizing today. Is it bigger than a breadbox but smaller than your car? Good! It's finally time to put to use all those shoeboxes, check register boxes, egg cartons, and wicker baskets you've hoarded throughout the years.

Step 3: Organize Your Stuff

It's time to get organized! Use items from your kitchen and office to contain the clutter you've sorted, keeping in mind that the most-used items should be easily accessible.

If you've done your homework properly, moving from Step 1 to Step 2, and didn't skip ahead to this step (Step 3), your organizing job isn't nearly as difficult as you thought it would be. This is where you assign a home for your treasured items to live, and to return to after they've been used.

Create zones or centers, much like in your child's classroom, to keep track of your household items. Common sense will play a big role here. Store tools in the basement or garage, arts & crafts supplies in the hobby room or kitchen, and extra paper towels in the kitchen pantry rather than under your bed.

Close your eyes, and picture yourself or your family using these household items. Walk through a typical day, thinking how and where you would use these items. Let's use Play-doh® as an example for how to decide where items should live.

Most parents store Play-Doh® in the toy chest or the closet shelf in their child's room, but it's a messy toy and perhaps should be used with adult supervision. As the manager of this home, where would *you* like to see your kids use Play-Doh®? At the kitchen table, where clay crumbs can easily be swept away with a broom and kept off the carpet? Or perhaps outside on the deck or patio?

By thinking clearly about where items are actually used, rather than stuffing them into leftover storage space, you are assigning a home and establishing a good future habit. Now each time you and Johnny work with clay, both of you will know where to return the Play-Doh®: to its rightful home on the upper shelf of whichever closet is closest to where the Play-Doh® will be used.

SIDE NOTE: Oddly enough, we think about childproofing cleaners and medicines, but not items such as pens, clay, paints, glues, and stickers. Of course it only takes one unplanned room-painting party to remind you that permanent markers are indeed permanent, and should be stored up high and remain off limits, used only with adult supervision.

Use this same visualization exercise with the remaining items in your "keep" stack when they present a storage dilemma. It's okay to think outside the box, and to store arts & crafts in the kitchen or laundry area not in the bedroom with other toys. Often storing medicines in the kitchen cabinet under lock and key makes much more sense for the parents of young children than stashing them in the traditional medicine cabinet.

Step 4: Maintain Your System On a Regular Basis

Keep up the hard work by maintaining your organizational system. This is perhaps the most challenging and overlooked step in organizing. It's fairly easy to *get* organized, but how on earth do you *stay* that way? Remember all those creative ideas you came up with in the **organizing step** of your project: file boxes, binders, and storage boxes? Those created a home for your papers and knick-knacks, and that's where you should continue to place incoming items on a regular basis. Don't let this organizing step overwhelm you - it's simply a matter of cleaning as you go, and making an effort to put things back where they belong.

Some efficiency experts feel that there is "a place for everything, and everything in its place." But that would be in a perfect world. My home certainly isn't perfect, and I'll bet yours isn't either! Instead of giving up before we even get started, let's walk through a typical day and its wonderful possibilities.

HOMEwork: Are you a Busybody?

2 Thessalonians 3: 11 says:

*For we hear that some among you are leading an
undisciplined life, doing no work at all but acting like
busybodies. Now such persons we command and exhort
in the Lord Jesus Christ to work in quiet fashion and
eat their own bread."*

Evaluate your own lifestyle. Are you a busybody
like Martha, creating clutter as fast as you can
clean it? Or are you an efficient home manager,
creating an atmosphere of calm and peace for
your family?

Use common sense organizing techniques to keep
your home safe and stress-free. Don't be afraid to
reorganize or move items around as the needs of
your family change. Obviously, as Junior grows
older, he can be trusted to refrain from marking
on the walls or using the blue toilet bowl cleaner
as finger paint.

Thinking *in the zone* helps with the long-term plan
of getting your household in order, making room
for baking, crafting, bill-paying and playing.
Since these are action words, we may as well call
your task centers ACTION ZONES.

The bill-paying action zone will probably be in
your kitchen rather than upstairs or at the back of
the house in the office. "Use it or lose it" applies
to organizing as well as brain cells. So set up your
newly organized house using common sense, as
well as the new skills you have learned. Believe
me, you'll thank yourself at the end of a long day.

Chapter Two:
Clutter Therapy for Your Home

Organize your home by practicing the **Four Basic Principles of Storage Solutions**:

1. Hang it Up.
2. Put it in a Drawer.
3. Store it on the Floor.
4. Shelf it.

If you use these four simple strategies, you can easily contain the clutter in a closet, garage, basement, bathroom, or playroom. The concepts are the same, and the containers don't need to be pricey. You can hang a bathroom towel on a shaker peg rack from the dollar store, or invest in an over-the-door rack from an upscale home décor catalog, depending on your budget and the resources that are available. But the results will be the same: the clutter is off the floor, out of the way, and has a new home to go to each and every day.

Titus 2:5 advises us to be sensible workers at home. Read verses 3-5:

"Older women likewise are to be reverent in their behavior, not malicious gossips, nor enslaved to much

wine, teaching what is good, that they may encourage the young women to love their husbands, to love their children, to be sensible, pure workers at home, kind, being subject to their own husbands, that the word of God may not be dishonored."

Bathroom:

Surviving the morning rush hour in any busy household is no easy feat, especially if you and your family are sharing bathroom space. Organizing tips for small spaces can quite easily reduce bathroom clutter. Utilize vertical space, minimize towel usage, and create a place for dirty clothes to reduce bathroom clutter in your home.

- **What's Your Bag** - Use a basket, over-the-door laundry bag, or a bag that hangs on the door knob to corral the clothes your family tosses away.
- **Throw In the Towel** - Assign each member of your family with a colored towel to be used more than once. If the thought of reusing a towel again gives your teenager the shudders, encourage her to at least use the same clean towel again and again to dry her hair.
- **Hang On** - Hang towels on hooks, shaker pegs, or over-the-door racks to conserve

space. Very few families I know of can actually get by with just those two built-in towel racks that came with the house!

- **Toss & Carry** – For clothes that aren't ready for laundering, implement the "toss-n-carry rule": you toss it, you carry it back to your bedroom as you leave.
- **Tween Rack™** – Hang a shaker peg or expandable hat rack in closets or on the door to accommodate clothes that are *in between* dirty and clean.
- **Going Up!** Use stacking bins, over-the-toilet shelves, hanging produce baskets or other stacking containers for toiletries in your shared space. Group like items together (towels, wash cloths, or shampoo), or assign one shelf/basket per family member.
- **This Is a Stick Up** – Use suction cups and adhesive tape to affix toothbrush holders, soap dishes, shampoo dispensers, and other bathroom organizers.

Bedroom:

1 Corinthians 6:19-20 reminds us that our body is a temple, and taking care of it by resting well is not only common sense but commanded by God.

"Or do you not know that your body is a temple of the Holy Spirit who is in you, whom you have from God, and that you are not your own? For you have been bought with a price: therefore glorify God in your body."

Ensure a good night's sleep by eliminating the clutter in your bedroom. Avoid working in your bedroom if at all possible, and try not to use your master suite as a storage facility for hobbies and canned goods. But if you are limited on space (and who isn't), hide what you can and then organize the rest. What you can't see can't hurt you!

- **Stash It** – Use under-the-bed storage tubs for out of season clothing, outgrown clothes, bill paying system, gift-wrap center, or to hide holiday gifts for the kids. This might be the only place to store pantry goods, so corral them into one sturdy container for easy retrieval. Be sure to use durable plastic as the cardboard boxes tend to attract pesky spiders and will eventually get stuck when those flimsy folding flaps wear out. Also, label the ends of the boxes so you can find that neatly organized stuff when you need it!
- **Behind Closed Doors** – Invest in a small inexpensive armoire to use as a home computer station, or a wardrobe to hide

your television and VCR. Sometimes you can add shelves to a small closet to achieve the same results.

- **Under the Mattress** – If your linen closet is small or nonexistent, try keeping a spare set of sheets tucked between your mattress and box springs. No need to run down the hall or to the bathroom closet for clean sheets.
- **Instant Work Station** – Store a piece of ply board under your bed to use as a work surface for hobbies. Placed on your mattress, it makes a wonderful cutting board for model airplanes, quilts, or scrap booking. When it's time for sleep, slip it under the bed, readjust the bed skirt, and your work will be out of sight.

Using this idea in a guest room makes double duty of the bedroom. When you don't have company, you can turn the room into a hobby area or home office. You can also quickly revert back into a bedroom again when guests arrive.

Family Room:

Use alternative organizing solutions to organize, disguise, and even hide the clutter created by your active family.

- **Screening Room** – A free-standing screen can be purchased from an import store, or

you can create your
own using piano hinges
and bi-fold doors.
Wicker, cloth, and
wood easily fit your
décor and lifestyle. Use
a screen to hide
playroom toys, a home office, or craft
projects.

- **Remote Roundup** – Corral remote controls, pens and paper inside a decorative box. Wooden cigar boxes, decoupage containers, or wicker holders can easily contain tabletop clutter on your coffee table or desktop. They double as child-proofers, too!

- **Basket Case** – Use wicker baskets and crates in various sizes and shapes to hold children's toys, games, magazines, and items to be put away in another room. Cubes easily stack to create a simple yet decorative play center for youngsters, and are easier on the eyes than plastic primary containers.   Form and function can co-exist!

Garage:

Whether you have the luxury of a
three-car garage or must store
cleaners and tools inside your

kitchen cupboard, **garage clutter** affects us all.
From attic to basement and beyond, no home
dweller is immune to the dilemma of where to
stash the solvents, glues, and drills. Using the
same organizing tips in the garage as you do in
the bathroom will contain the clutter and keep
you from dreading those honey-dos around your
house (well, almost!)

- Hang wooden lathe stripes horizontally
  around the inside walls of your garage, add
  large nails or hooks, and viola! You have an
  instant and expensive way to organize
  long-handled tools.
- Use bike hooks to hang your cycles from
  the ceiling and get them out of your car's
  way.
- Mount a large pegboard on the wall, add
  hooks, and you're ready for any DIY
  project. (Be sure to leave about ¼ inch
  between the board and wall so that the
  hooks can grip the peg hole.)
- Scour the garbage piles in your
  neighborhood on trash pick-up day (or visit
  some garage sales) for kitchen cupboard
  cast offs. Old kitchen cupboards and
  countertops make excellent garage
  organizers and are usually free for the
  taking.
- Mount jar lids to the underside of garage
  shelves or cabinets, and then screw in the

matching jar for instant and clutter free organizers. Once limited to breakable baby food jars, you're now free to use margarine tubs and plastic peanut butter jars to ensure garage safety for your handyman and his little helpers.

- Utilize wide-mouthed tubs and cans for tape, coils of wire, and screws.
- Invert an old barstool to corral mops, brooms, rakes and shovels. Works for sporting goods such as hockey sticks, skis, fishing poles and baseball bats, too!

Kids' Rooms:

For younger children, create **action zones** or centers like the ones they use at daycare or elementary school. For older children, use the following as a foundation but gear it more toward privacy and entertaining their friends rather than creative play:

- Sleeping (bed, pillow, nightlight, stuffed animals)
- Music (radio, cassettes or CDs, headphones, battery charger).
- Watching TV or videos (bean bag chair or overstuffed bed pillow, remote controls, VHS tapes, tape organizer).

- Computing (sturdy table, ergonomic chair, foot rest, mouse pad, games and educational software, a shelf on which to store software) .
- Homework (chair, table or desk, task lighting, pencil, paper, research materials).
- Reading (overstuffed chair, floor cushion, or bean bag; floorlamp or task lighting).
- Housekeeping (table & chairs, kitchen, dishes, play food, vacuum or broom, various props for creative play for little girls and boys).
- Dramatic play (dress-up clothes on hooks or in a box, mirror, puppets).
- Science (aquarium or terrarium for fish/turtle/lizard & pet food, shelf or small table for collections, explorer kit (microscope, telescope, binoculars, flashlight, compass, magnet, magnifying glass)).
- Blocks (quiet place to build block towers and cities, preferably carpeted for noise reduction, various sizes and shapes of blocks in wood, plastic, sturdy cardboard).
- Carpet time (plenty of floor space to play with dolls, cars, or action figures).

Kitchen:

The universal complaint I hear from mothers everywhere is that they don't have enough storage space in their kitchens. But did you know that only 20% of the items in your kitchen are used 80% of the time? That means that you don't use a lot of that kitchen stuff, so maybe it's time to get rid of duplicate measuring cups and unused wedding gifts (what DOES that salad shooter do, anyway?) Good news: I'm going to let you keep your junk drawer! Provided you promise to clean it out once every month or so, you can fill 'er up to your heart's content. No need to go overboard throwing everything away and becoming a minimalist this early in your organizing quest, but do take it easy on hoarding twist-ties and rubber bands, okay?

- **Stack It Up** – Utilize racks in your cupboards to organize dinner plates, serving platters, and bowls. No longer expensive and hard to find, these plastic-coated wire racks can be found in most home improvement and discount stores. They'll literally double your storage space so you can squeeze in more dishes and avoid chipping the ones you have.
- **The Spice of Life** – Organize spices and seasonings by storing them in door-mounted racks, expandable shelves, and small baskets. From allspice to vanilla, you can keep those little bottles and jars from hiding if you corral them in a small container of their own. Shoeboxes, drawer organizers, and plastic tubs with missing

lids make affordable organizing solutions
for your pantry and cupboard.

- **Out of the Box** – Most of us have received
decorative spice racks or canisters during
our homemaking days, but who really has
been able to find the wall or counter space
for these things? And they seem to be one
more thing to dust, too! Why not think out-
of-the-box and get creative when you
organize your dried goods? Use airtight
plastic containers for sugar, flour, coffee,
and tea. Pour rice and cereal into taller
containers that have a spout for easy
pouring. If you're particular about the look
of your pantry, then splurge on fancy name
brand containers in uniform sizes. But if
you live in the real world with the rest of
us, I hereby give you permission to reuse
whipped cream and ice cream tubs with
their lids. (I personally got a lot of mileage
out of Chinese take-out containers once
used for egg drop soup—the lids fit
perfectly with no spills and even kept foods
fresh in the freezer. I think mine finally
died an agonizing death after 8 years.)

- **Just Hangin' Around** – Create an instant
pantry from the broom closet, coat closet, or
a smaller version inside a cupboard door.
Hang an over-the-door organizer on a
closet door to create a wonderful space for
cans, boxes, and envelopes. Smaller
shelving racks hold spices or transform a

cabinet door into a medicine cabinet in an
instant (and they're out of children's reach,
too).

- **Top of the Mornin' to You** – Transform
that dead space atop your refrigerator into
a bookcase. Move those ugly cereal boxes
(caught you, didn't I!) to another cabinet
and store your cookbooks in a clean dry
spot. I have mine in a long rectangular
basket, but you can easily contain yours
with heavy bookends. Store your seldom
used picnic basket up here, filled with a
picnic-on-the-go kit that's ready for sun,
fun, and guaranteed rain.
- **Pretty and Functional** – Not enough
drawer space? Scoop up those wooden
spoons and spatulas and store them in a
pretty ceramic pitcher or crock. Store
napkins, paper plates, and plastic ware in a
picnic basket. Use wicker baskets to hold
paperwork, bills to be paid, and kids'
permission slips.
- **Fridge Clutter** – Consolidate all those little
pictures on the front of your refrigerator
with a magnetic photo mat, or acrylic
magnet frames. Trade in the retail magnets
holding notes and reminder cards for a
single magnetic clip (heavy duty). Clip a
four-color pen on the family calendar and
hang with two magnetic clips for easy
scheduling. Retire those falling magnetic
ABC's and replace them with an alphabet

poster that has adhesive magnets mounted
on the back.

HOMEwork -

Name three creative ways the following items can
be used to store stuff in your home:

- Tiered Vegetable Basket
- Wooden Cigar Box
- Film Canister
- Makeup Bag
- Zippered Pencil Case
- 3-Ring Notebook
- Dishwashing Tub
- Plastic Coat Hanger
- Plastic Milk Crate
- Wooden Peg Rack
- Plastic Shoe Shelf
- Canvas Book Bag
- Over-the-Door Shoe Bag

(Suggestions can be found in the back of this
workbook, **but there are no right or wrong
answers.**)

Daydreaming Exercise – Profile of the Perfect Day

Take a moment to stop and daydream. Rather than a frantic morning that gets everyone's day off to a bumpy start, visualize the way you want your day to start. How 'bout this?

After your shower, you use the last of your tube of toothpaste, so you make a note on the toiletry **inventory sheet** hanging inside your linen closet door to purchase more. While fixing breakfast, you realize you're almost out of milk and eggs, so you jot down those items on your **grocery list**, which is posted on the side of your fridge. You come into the kitchen to see your family gathered and sitting – dressed and ready – at the table because clothes were cleaned, pressed and laid out the night before. Everyone is now able to sit down and enjoy a calm breakfast.

Lunches were prepared the night before and stuffed neatly into backpacks so no one misses their car pool or school bus. Homework was completed last night and added to the packs that hang on the coat rack. Videos can be returned on time to the video store on the way to work because you and your spouse tossed them into the **out box** last night as soon as you finished watching them.

Everybody is up, dressed, fully prepared, and out the door on time to start their day in an orderly and utterly delightful manner!

This may truly seem like a fairy tale, but many parts of this scene can be played out in your own home if you use the organizing steps outlined in this workbook. Now... on with making your dream a reality!

Debbie's Alternative Organizing Solutions™ For Maintaining an Organized Home:

- **Grab-n-Go Bag™**: A home version of an **out box**. Fill with outbound items such as library books, videos, dry cleaning, mail, and other necessities you will need as you run routine errands. Fill as you go to avoid scurrying back home to get those items you forgot.
- **Out Box**: It works in your office, why not try out boxes at home? One per family member to keep track of important papers in the kitchen or home office. Or label boxes/trays for: Bills to Pay, Papers to Sign, Papers to File, and Articles to Read.
- **Tween Rack™:** A simple rack with hooks or pegs for those items that are 'tween dirty and clean. Hang one in the bathroom for reusable towels, inside the closet for play clothes or workout gear, and one in the coat closet or mudroom for backpacks.

- **Remote Roundup**: Use a decorative box to corral remote controls and the TV guide. Whether it's a wooden cigar box or a handmade decoupage container, you'll now have a home for all those "clickers." It's a great tool for childproofing the coffee table or hiding living room clutter before company comes.

- **Simple Forms:** Use a spreadsheet to create templates for tracking things you've ordered by mail or phone, comparison-shopping of major purchases, or to inventory your household items. One form can be modified for videos, VHS tapes, CDs, online orders, and so forth. You can even make a list for groceries, discount stores, and other things you need to take care of.

- **Family Calendar**: If a planner doesn't work for your family's scheduling needs, then it's time to color your world with stickers or ink on the family calendar. Post your calendar using heavy-duty magnets on the refrigerator, clip on a four-color ink pen, and you'll know at a glance who should be where (and when). Assign one color per family member, or a color for a certain type of activity - it doesn't matter *how* you do it just as long as you're consistent.

For instance, RED is a doctor appointment, BLUE is sports, GREEN is school activity for the kids, BLACK is volunteer work. Don't forget to enlighten the rest of the members of your family about your new system or it'll be useless!

My Blessing for You

"Have a long life, peace be to you, and peace be to your house, and peace be to all that you have." — 1 Samuel 25: 6

Chapter Three:
It's About Time

In this part of the course, we'll be discussing the *Five Steps to Becoming an Effective Time Manager*. The definition of a home manager is exactly what it sounds like. You soon will be able to incorporate the same time management tools learned at work to manage your home. Obviously it is a little harder to delegate work to your household staff, especially when they are less than three feet tall and like to talk back! But as we learn about the five steps, I'll provide you with practical tips on how you can run your home just as smoothly as any business.

You'll learn how to:

Step 1 - **Prioritize** your tasks instead of making a running list so that you can use goals to get things accomplished.

Step 2 - **Delegate** effectively because you are just one person and it's too hard to be split too many ways.

Step 3 - **Limit interruptions**. It's not a myth- it's reality.

Step 4 - **Consolidate** tasks.

Step 5 - **Use time blocks** for optimum organization.

Perhaps you are thinking this is common sense, that you learned this in a business class, or that you already use these skills at work—and that's wonderful! During this course you will learn organizing tips to use in the trenches with your family so that you will be able to rely upon someone beside yourself to get umpteen things accomplished.

Philippians 4:6 tells us to:

> *"be anxious for nothing, but in everything by prayer and supplication with thanksgiving let your requests be made known to God."*

Proverbs 16:3 states:

> *"Commit your works to the Lord,*
> *And your plans will be established."*

Now let's discuss the **Five Steps to Becoming an Effective Time Manager**. I'll introduce the steps briefly for now, and when we take a break you can think of ways that you can customize this system for your own household.

Step 1: Prioritizing

The Right Tools for the Job

You can use simple tools to prioritize your day
such as a "to do" list. If you're not a list maker,
then use a family calendar (which by the way is
used by 90% of the readers polled on my website
at Organizedtimes.com). It's easy to use and is an
effective way to see where you need to be and
with whom.

If you already own a comprehensive planner, such
as a PDA, that's wonderful — please don't stop
using what works. But if you have found that
what you've been using in the past isn't working,
don't feel like the Queen of the Organizationally
Challenged and give up hope. It merely means
that you need to modify your system or change it
entirely to reflect your new lifestyle.

Confession from a professional organizer: I've
changed time management systems several times
in the past five years as my organizing needs have
changed. As a new full-time mother, I purchased a
small notebook planner to store in my diaper bag
or purse, then switched to computer software
when I spent most of my time online in my home
business. As my son became involved in
preschool, and I got involved with outside
activities again, I switched to an electronic planner

that could be tossed into my purse or tote bag and synchronized with my computer's software. Now that I am speaking and spending more time in the field away from my computer, I am going back to the smaller sized planner. But as I travel more, I am tempted by the PDAs that deliver email and Internet sites right to your handheld device—I just love having access to that technology!

For those of you who have worked in a position where you were responsible to one or more bosses, you probably realize all too well how difficult it can be to make do with someone else's system. Perhaps as a new employee you entered this position with some training. The trainer shared that "this is how we do it around here; it works great the way it is, and you shouldn't have to change a thing." But after a week of struggling with *the system*, you might realize that it's not working for *you*.

Managing your home is much the same. Notice I didn't say to manage your **family**— you're not trying to organize your husband. (It doesn't work! Believe me, I've been married 18 years and I *know* it doesn't – I've tried unsuccessfully in the past.) Just as wives realize that we can't change our husbands but can change our expectations, so too can we manage our home.

Rank and File:

Another thing you can do to prioritize and
manage your tasks is to keep your list short and
manageable. Try to rank or group your "to dos"
by A, B, or C priority. (Bear with me if this is a
simple thing to understand; not everyone has had
the benefit of time management training so I like
to start with the basics to make sure you are with
me. It's a very simple concept once you've used it
for awhile.)

When making a list, you first need to determine
the most important thing you have to do today.
Assign it a ranking of **A or #1**. Color-code it on
your list or calendar with a pen or stickers to
make it easy to read. Make sure it's portable so
that you can grab it and go. Then you won't have
to dismantle it from the fridge, and try to take
everything with you while flying out the door
when you leave to run errands.

Do the same thing with your **B or #2** priorities.
These are things that don't necessarily have to be
done first during the day, but that should get
accomplished. An example of a B priority is going
to the dry cleaners. Your husband may be almost
out of work shirts, and it's time to go to the dry
cleaners today. If you can't make it today, but can
go first thing tomorrow morning, then that will
work, too.

The **C or #3** priorities are usually the last thing on *my* list, and I'm lucky if I get them done during the course of a week much less every single day! In the course of your day, a C priority might be cleaning out the kitchen junk drawer. Most of us bump this from day to day to day. It IS something that needs to get done, but only when you have nothing else pressing to do.

Bill paying is definitely an A priority, whereas organizing your closet or cleaning out your junk drawer- taking care of things that are not mandatory- would be B and C priorities.

If you are easily distracted, have ADD, or are constantly interrupted, consider using an index card system. Write one item on each index card (3x5 inches or 5x7 inches), group with other tasks, and secure with a rubber band or store inside a recipe box. If you really like things out in plain sight, mount a bulletin board on a wall or near your refrigerator, or wherever you know it will be used, and spread out the cards so that you can see what your "to do" list is at a glance.

Your time management system doesn't have to be in a fancy binder, and you don't have to pay for expensive training. You should keep your system portable. Don't just go out and invest money and time to create a new system and then let it gather dust in your purse, car or on your countertop.

Take the extra effort to make it work. Try to give it three weeks before giving up on yourself.

Efficiency experts who study human behavior have discovered that it takes an average of 21 days (3 weeks) to create or discontinue a habit. So maybe you're stopping an old habit and then creating a new one. In that case it takes about three weeks to find out if this new system is really working for you. If not, then it's time to reevaluate it, change something that's not working, and then modify it. Resist the temptation to give up on it completely.

Step 2: Delegating

The second characteristic of an effective home manger is **delegating**. As a mother, woman, wife, business owner, work at home mom, or volunteer you *must* share the load. One thing I'd like to convey to you is that *you're not alone.* Your family is a unit or team working together for the common good. When you delegate tasks to be done, you're not only sharing responsibility to free yourself to do more things, but you are being an effective manager.

Most of us learn, by being a manager or by working for one, that the boss does a lot of work. Most of that work is supervisory. He makes sure that the majority of the work gets done. The CEO

of McDonald's is not behind the counter flipping
burgers or making French fries. Instead, he's
making sure his managers are in the stores getting
things done and taking care of the customers.
Good production and service is a true reflection of
his managerial skills so he makes sure his ship
runs smoothly. If he tried to do every single thing
that needed doing within the company, *nothing
would be done effectively.* You wouldn't enjoy the
taste of the fries, your child might be missing
some toys in her Happy Meals™, and there would
be a lot of things falling through the cracks. We all
need to share the load.

You never know what you'll get until you ask.
You are surrounded by people that you love — and
with children that love is unconditional. They just
don't know any better than to pitch in and help.
Preschoolers and toddlers love to help. When
they chip in, be sure to make their tasks age
appropriate. I know the thought of one more
confrontation with your teenager gives you the
shudders, but if you can use your creativity to
make her think she is special and you really need
her help, she just may surprise you.

Get kids involved in the planning, perhaps
through participation in a family meeting. Put
your heads together to decide what needs doing,
when, and by whom. This helps tremendously in
the overall household system, because you are
treating your kids like they almost have a brain,

like a little adult. (Of course they think they're adults anyway!) You of course know who's really in charge, and by the time they figure out what's going on, it'll be too late — those positive habits will already be established.

Proverbs 22:6 reminds us to:

> *"Train up a child in the way he should go,*
> *Even when he is old he will not depart from it."*

I'll give you a prime example of never knowing what you'll get until you ask for it. I've been married for 18 years to a wonderful man, who also happens to be a packrat (I mean collector... his personal term of choice). It makes my job as an organizer very challenging to "walk my talk," and slows me down when I have to ask first before tossing things away.

But when I began asking for help with routine tasks such as making dinner or babysitting for an hour on Saturdays to give me a break, my job became much easier. As wives and mothers we've learned to give and give without end. We don't take time for ourselves, and may become passive aggressive. But most people can read the resentment reflected in your face and in your body language. Remember: It's not what you say, it's how you say it. The passive aggression can

lead to resentment, and the resentment to
bitterness. Ask for help when you need it!

Another delegating tool that has worked very well
in my household is the chore chart. This works
not just for the children but also for the adults.
We can all see what needs to be done, and who
needs to do it. If a chore is not getting done, we
can all use our noodles to figure out why.

Maybe David, who is in charge of taking out
trash, is too young at age five to do this each day
so Dad can start doing it. But David can certainly
take over Dad's responsibility of feeding the cat
each morning instead. Things are now
accomplished, no one is overworked, and it was a
fairly easy solution to the problem.

Read Ephesians 6: 1-4, focusing on verse 4:

> *"and fathers, do not provoke your children to
> anger; but bring them up in the discipline and
> instruction of the Lord."*

Obviously, you can substitute the word "mother"
for "father" in this verse. I am a firm believer that
our life's mission as parents is to raise our
children to be independent and as accountable
citizens of God's world. He has entrusted us with
this precious gift, and it's up to us to provide
guidance and instruction in a loving manner (not

by nagging or criticizing). Using positive reinforcers such as charting and incentives is one way to do just that.

Don't forget this not-so-gentle reminder from King Solomon about nagging:

Proverbs 21: 9, 19

> *"It is better to live in a corner of a roof,*
> *Than in a house shared with a contentious*
> *woman.*
>
> *It is better to live in a desert land,*
> *Than with a contentious and vexing woman."*

HOMEwork: Create a Family Chore Chart

- **Take** a break, grab a pad of paper, and make a list of the household chores that need to be done on a regular basis. Group them by frequency: daily, twice weekly, weekly, twice monthly, monthly, quarterly, twice yearly, and yearly. This isn't gospel, it's just a guide or starting point for your family's work schedule. Review your list and make either a mental note or underline those chores that can be done less often and still maintain a level of cleanliness in your household.

- **Tell** your husband that you need to have a business meeting with him, and schedule a good time for you both to discuss the new game plan, say for about 15 minutes. Believe me, this is well worth the wait — who can concentrate on creating a new routine for their kids when the big game is on television or he's in the middle of balancing the checkbook? Then review your list of chores *together*, tweaking it until it's a list you both can live with.

- **Schedule** a family meeting to discuss the new Family Chore Chart. Schedule a time when each member in your family (this includes grandparents, foreign exchange students, and dads, too) can attend to discuss changes in your household.

- **Present** your plan to the rest of the family, complete with a large version of the list on poster board or individual lists for each person to read. Bring a Chore Chart (either hand made or purchased from a teacher supply store) to the meeting as a visual prop for everyone to see.

- **Assign** chores to your family based on volunteers and assignments that are appropriate for age and ability. For instance: toddlers can dust, feed animals, make their bed, and help empty the dishwasher. Grade school children can empty trashcans, weed the garden, water the plants, set the table. Middle school kids can put out the trash, load recyclables into the car or van, mow the lawn, rake leaves, and vacuum. High school kids can help with laundry, clean out gutters, walk or drive younger children to school/pick them up from school. I'm sure you will easily come up with the first draft of your new system.

- **List** the chores and the name of the person responsible for doing them on the Chore Chart. Write it in pencil or erasable ink, or use a wipe-off board—I'm sure you'll be changing these in the months to come.

- **Discuss** the rewards and consequences of responsibilities with your children. Whether you use stickers, checkmarks, or smiley faces on your chart is totally up to you, but use something that everyone likes to see on a daily basis to remind them to get their work done.

Proverbs 22: 6, 15 encourages us to discipline our children:

> *Train up a child in the way he should go,*
> *Even when he is old he will not depart from it."*
>
> *Foolishness is bound up in the heart of a child;*
> *The rod of discipline will remove it far from*
> *him."*

Quite often verse 15 is taken out of context by parents who do not believe in spanking their children. The word discipline, according to Webster's New Riverside Dictionary is defined as:

"to train or develop by teaching or control" and "to impose order on." Children need structure!

- **Establish** a point system that is age appropriate, and be consistent with it. For instance, don't expect a toddler to do a lot of chores, or a preschooler to go all week before getting a reward—their little minds can't think that far ahead and by the time they get a treat for being good, they'll forget what it was for!

  My son, for example, is five and we've been charting his chores since he was three. Prior to that, it was verbal and he got a sticker/ treat for each task he completed throughout the day and a treat at the day's end. After a few weeks, as he learned the system and became a little more mature, we tapered him to a daily treat with only stickers for each task.

Then at age three and a half we started the Chore Chart, using the system already in place. He has three chores on his chart (which are blocked off Monday through Sunday, one square per day), and they are changed as he grows or to reflect the "issue of the hour."

When we began, he was waking us up at 5:00 each morning ready for the new day, so his chart included: Being Quiet in the Morning, Feeding the Cat, and Putting Away Toys. We worked together on each task (he was, after all, only three!), and then he got instant feedback when the task was done. If he balked at doing any of these chores/responsibilities, he got an X on his chart and didn't get his treat at the end of the day.

When he reached a belligerent (talking back) stage a few months later, we added a Bonus Chore: if he could go all day long without going into time out, he got a bonus regardless of the day's progress. If he was sick, we were traveling, or he just had a

bad day, he could still earn some sort of
incentive. And it took out almost all of the
emotional baggage that goes with
disciplining a preschooler!

Now at age five, he has four chores and his
bonus: Put Away Toys, Stay Quiet in the
Morning (still an issue for my little early
bird), Feed the Cat, and Make the Bed. And
he still has the bonus of no time outs.

Here's the breakdown on the points system
for our family:

- Each time David completes a chore, he
  gets to put a sticker on his chart. (I
  post the chart high in case he decides
  to get creative and embellish it
  himself.)
- After dinner when he picks up toys, if
  he has earned all his stickers he gets a
  treat from the treasure box. Then I
  add 1 point to his weekly total.
- At the end of the day, if he has not
  gone into time out, he earns a bonus
  point and he gets another treat. No
  whining, no exceptions.
- IF he does his work, THEN he gets
  paid.
- When he has accumulated 14 points
  he gets a special treat of his choosing:
  a trip to the dollar store for a toy, a

visit to the playground at McDonald's, a special play date, or something else that he values as a treat.

We started our weekly points at five, then moved it gradually to seven, then twelve, now it's at fourteen). He may not get his points earned each week, and then sometimes he has a great week and the points just fly up on that chart! It all depends on him, and he alone can change it. Each day's progress is discussed with praise and encouragement.

This is called **positive parenting**, or positive reinforcement. I've used it in my classroom with 33 kindergarteners and no teacher's aids, and I now use it successfully in my own home. And the beauty of it is that it keeps us consistent, less emotional, and on task. (Sorry for the pun — couldn't resist!). I think it will work for you and your family, too.

Step 3: Limiting Interruptions

This is the third characteristic of an effective home manager. It's a very important tool of time management. It works in an office environment and I promise it will work in your home if you

stick with it and enforce your family rules.
Do you drop off the kids at school and then arrive
at work only to complain of how hectic your
weekend was? Or do you cringe each time the
doorbell rings right as your family sits down to
dinner?

Proverbs 14: 1 reminds us:

> *"The wise woman builds her house,*
> *But the foolish tears it down with her own*
> *hands."*

You are in control of your household, not your
children or the other person on the other end of
the phone or other side of the door.

Proverbs 24: 3-4 promises:

> *"By wisdom a house is built,*
> *And by understanding it is established;*
> *And by knowledge the rooms are filled*
> *With all precious and pleasant riches."*

I recommend that you manage your home as you
would manage your office. Concentrate on the
tasks that you're doing now, and block out all the
other distractions. Begin with simple time
management techniques such as these:

1.) Don't Have An Open Door Policy

Screen phone calls and don't answer the door during restricted times. Stick to your house rules. Maybe the rule for your family is that you don't answer the door during dinnertime. Or you don't allow phone calls during homework time. This may sound strict, but if you are having a tough time managing your time, and that of your children, then it's imperative that you have a plan and stick with it.

If you try this system 2-3 weeks and it doesn't work, by all means change it a bit. Back off a little and limit the phone calls to a shorter time rather than not at all. Your children's friends will still be there after dinner and they can always be called back. But you can't recapture that family time when you discuss what's going on in everyone's lives, from the mundane (Mom, I'm out of blue jeans) to the critical (I need a prom dress by tomorrow, Mom)! Take advantage of closing the virtual door and not having an open door policy in your organized home.

If you work from home, the same time management principle applies. Don't answer the door to a solicitor if you're busy working on a report or typing a business plan. Multitasking or doing more than one thing at a time is good if you're not going to compromise the effectiveness of one of those tasks. That means if you need to just do one thing at a time and do it well, it's a good time to implement that rule.

2.) Use Power Tools Wisely

Let your voicemail, caller i.d. or answering machine be your personal secretary to screen phone calls for you. Maybe you have a new baby at your house. In between trying to feed and clothe the older three kids, taking care of the new arrival, and answering phone calls from friends and family, you find yourself sleep deprived and running on empty. You can't take care of your baby and family, much less yourself. This is a wonderful opportunity to take advantage of that modern technology at your service.

Record an outgoing voicemail announcement such as: "We have a new baby girl/boy!" Then provide callers with your baby's name and birth statistics (height, weight, etc.). "Baby, mommy, and daddy are doing fine. Please give us [insert a time period here, such as 3 days, 1 week, etc.] to settle in and then we'll be receiving visitors." If you're really creative, this is a good time to make the baby's first web site. Send photos over the Internet or

via email to family members who are too far
away to see the new arrival. This option
provides you and your spouse some breathing
room while still keeping in touch with friends
and family who can't wait to hear the exciting
news about your bundle of joy.

3.) Learn to Say No!

Do you suffer from "OverVolunteer-itis"? Do
you find yourself spending more time at the
school than at home? Or perhaps you are
always the first one the ladies call to bake
cookies for the church bazaar but you don't
even own a cookie sheet!

Consider this passage in Romans 12: 3- 8:

*"For through the grace given to me I say to every
man among you not to think more highly of himself
than he ought to think; but to think so as to have
sound judgment, as god has allotted to each a
measure of faith.*

*For just as we have many members in one body and
all the members do not have the same function,
So we who are many, are one body in Christ, and
individually members one of another.
And since we have gifts that differ according to the
grace given to us, let each exercise them
accordingly: if prophesy, according to the
proportion of his faith;*

*If service, in his serving; or he who teaches, in his
teaching;*

*Or he who exhorts, in his exhortation; he who gives,
with liberality; he who leads, with diligence, he who
shows mercy, with cheerfulness."*

This passage explains our relationship as believers
to the body of the Church, each with a role to play
for God's glory. Pay particular attention to verse
6:

*... And since we have gifts that differ according to
the grace given to us, let each exercise them
accordingly...*

Claim this verse each time you feel guilty about
saying "no" to your son's teacher, the PTA
chairman, or your Sunday school teacher. You
aren't saying "no" to GOD, but to a man (or
woman). We are each given a talent and must
focus on what we do best.

And if you're still unsure about saying no, read 1
Corinthians 13 and Galatians 6:3-5. These passages
should give you the strength to say no to those
who judge your willingness to serve.

I am hereby giving you permission not to be
Super Mom! So you can turn off your cell phone
and mute your beeper (or set it to vibrate). Try not

to focus on those interruptions, not only for yourself but also for those around you. Maybe during dates with your husband you really do need to be accessible to the babysitter. But if you're feeling stressed and need to visit with your best friend over morning coffee, turn off your beeper or cell phone. If you're with the kids in the park, this is a great time to turn off the whole world to focus entirely on them. It's not written anywhere in the "Manual Of Womanhood" that you have to be accessible 24/7!

The same thing holds true for emails. Just because you receive an email you don't have to drop whatever you're doing to go respond, especially if you're in the middle of dinner, are concentrating on a business report, or helping the kids with their homework.

You need to focus on the task at hand, whatever you're doing at the time. Try to filter out these interruptions by using timesaving tools, not having an open door policy, and just saying no.

HOMEwork- Limiting Interruptions

Based on what you have learned about limiting interruptions, complete the worksheet **Limiting Interruptions** below. Use the three methods

CONTROLLING INTERRUPTIONS

Type of Interruption	Method of Control

discussed earlier (no open door policy, use of power tools, saying no), or implement your own.

Step 4: Consolidate Tasks

The fourth characteristic of an effective time manager is the ability to consolidate tasks. This may sound simple to someone who is not trying to run a household. But by consolidating your errands and routine tasks, you will find hidden time that you didn't even know you had. We all find ourselves saying, "I had no time this weekend. We spent all day Saturday running the kids from soccer to baseball to gymnastics, and then we had to run errands." (And we wonder why our kids are cranky and acting out. Hmmmm.....)

I recommend that you limit your interruptions during the day (such as phone calls, emails and voicemails) as recommended earlier so that you can focus on what you're working on at the time. Then consolidate the rest and tackle them in either a single time block or a couple of smaller ones at your convenience.

For example, you probably shouldn't take a phone call while writing a report or balancing your checkbook, as phone calls interrupt the creative flow. But when you've finished your A priority (the checkbook), you can then return all those

missed calls in one sitting. Many of us do this
successfully in a business environment but
wouldn't consider doing this at home. Maybe it's
time to give it a try.

Let's say that it's Lauren's turn to write down all
the phone messages you received during dinner.
Your teenage son's friends called, telemarketers
began their relentless pursuit, your mother called,
your husband's coworker phoned.... the list goes
on and on. Have Lauren write down all those
messages so that you can organize them and
process them. Are you going to return the calls
after washing dishes or wait until tomorrow
morning? If you are going to call them all back at
once, whom do you call first? How do you
prioritize all those callbacks?

The process you use depends on your personal
preference, but I would venture to say that work-
related messages take a higher precedence over
those of your child's friends. A call to a family
member who needs a lot of TLC (tender loving
care) may be reserved for a time when you can
chat privately for awhile. Maybe you decide it's
first come, first served. Perhaps the person who
called earlier will be handled before the one who
called later and then it's on to #2, #3, and #4. Or
you can prioritize that which is most important to
you. You, as the home manager, are the *best* one to
decide which system will work for you and your

family. This recommendation may sound vague, but it really depends on your personal schedule as to how you handle it.

Another task to consolidate is errands. Most of us do this already without realizing it, so I hope this serves as a gentle reminder. Unless you experience cabin fever if you don't get out on a daily basis, do try to limit your errand-running to one or two days each week rather than every day. Not only will you conserve gas, but you will also cut down on commute time as well. We generally limit thoughts of commuting to a corporate environment; yet going to the dry cleaners during parenting hours is based on the same concept. So when you consolidate your tasks, remember that some commute time is dead time and can be better used in more effective ways.

Step 5: Time Blocks

The fifth characteristic of an effective time manager is being able to use time blocks. Take your #1 or A priority tasks and finish those first. If you want to do them all at once then utilize one big time block to give yourself peace of mind. Or allow 10-15 minutes for a B priority. This will vary with your list, from day to day. Those 15 minutes really do add up over the course of time!

For example, if you have several errands to run in places all over town, obviously you will need to save some of your "to do's" for tomorrow (or the next errand day in your schedule); and that's just fine. You don't have to accomplish each and everything on your "to do" list. Did you read that correctly? You sure did! I hereby give you permission NOT to complete your "to do" list.

That means you don't have to stay up until two a.m. folding towels, and you certainly don't need to run 20 errands in one single day, exhausting your gas tank and yourself! In fact, one of my clients told me she was so frustrated with her current schedule that just being able to cross *one* thing off her "to do" list each day was a major milestone. She had set her standards so high that she didn't know where to start (or where to stop, either).

HOMEwork: Time Wasters and Time Savers

I'd like to share some bonus tips with you that I call **time wasters**. They fall under the category of interruptions, appointments, errands, chores, parenting, and time management.

Problem: Let's say your biggest time waster of the day is interruptions such as the doorbell or telephone. Unless you live in a cave, you will have lots of interruptions, there's just no getting around it.

Solution: Have an interruption policy where you screen your visitors and consolidate your phone calls so you don't have those interruptions. Enforce the family rules such as no calls during dinner, no calls after 8 pm, and no calls during study time. Remain in control of the chaos creators in your family's life.

Problem: Perhaps your time waster is keeping too many appointments, and you feel as if you are constantly waiting on someone.

Solution: Keep your appointments brief, say 10-15 minutes. This appointment might be with your mother, best friend, or baby sitter.

Schedule appointments with dentists, doctors, and other service providers during the first part of the day so that you don't fall victim to the doctor's schedule running behind. Call ahead to see if they are running on schedule so you won't have to wait on them. If they are running behind, ask what time you are likely to be seen and come at that time.

Schedule appointments during slow times. You may need to get really creative for this one, and it may sound like common sense to you, but it really does help. For example, don't visit the mall on Saturday or Sunday when the stores are at their busiest. Go to the grocery store late in evening, or early in the morning (especially on weekends).

Those of us with young children can't sleep late, but others can! Most people are sleeping in and not thinking about grocery shopping on Saturday morning. Try to avoid the post office on Mondays and Fridays. Don't schedule doctor appointments on Mondays or Fridays either. Try to get everything done in mid-week when others are not bombarding service providers with their needs. You'll achieve much more, and reduce stress while you're at it.

Multitask when you can, which means doing more than one thing at once. If you are kept waiting and find yourself growing impatient, make sure you are prepared. For example, perhaps you're waiting to be seen by your OB/ GYN for a routine exam. A woman comes in who is having an emergency. It can't be helped but obviously you're routine exam will have to wait until the emergency is under control. This is a great time to get out your Christmas card list to address envelopes (even if it is only October), or to catch up on letter writing. You can do both if you carry a tote bag filled with "boredom supplies". Whether you spending the time cross-stitching or reading a novel— be prepared and be productive!

Problem: Running errands seems to be a never-ending part of your life.

Solution: When you run errands, try to consolidate them (as we discussed earlier). Also, plan your route. Or if you're going to a place you've never been before, photocopy your city map, take your highlighter, and trace your route. It helps tremendously to serve as your own personal navigator.

If you're just running errands in town, try to avoid running back and forth. I actually know some people who visit the dry cleaners, return home to pick up videos only to double back to the video store next door to the cleaners! Try to create a route where you're not crisscrossing over your path too many times.

Keep a tote bag or plastic tub in your coat closet or by your front door for outgoing things. Now you can grab it, and head right out the door for a quick trip to errand-land.

Problem: Chores are a big time-waster, so I encourage you to get help with these. Try to keep communication at the forefront of your master "to do" list.

Solution: Call a family meeting to establish who does what and when. When you do so, your family will actually help you create that "to do" list. This is a good example of communicating rather than assuming you know what they need.

Lower your expectations a little. For instance, my husband doesn't care if I vacuum weekly. Every two weeks or even monthly is just fine with him. Talking with him about his take on the chores and how often they should be done has enabled me to focus on things that we all benefit from, such as baking. (He would rather I bake than vacuum any day!) My husband is continuously helping me to establish my priorities.

This is something a good manager does on a regular basis. Unless you are the top manager of a corporation, you will answer to somebody at some level. When you are faced with frustration and go to your boss for help, you are in effect practicing good time management skills. You say, " I can't do all this. You gave me twelve things to do and I only have time for five. I need help!" At some point you will have to decide whether to fall apart or ask for help to get things done. A good manager will then take your task list and say, "Okay, let's give these three things to Ernie, these four things to Paula, these four things to you, and I'll do this one." Divide and conquer!

You can do the same thing as a home manager. Hand it right back to your children and spouse so they can figure out what needs to be done, what can wait, and how well it needs doing. There's no rush to do everything at once, just use little time blocks here and there. When your family thinks it's time to get something accomplished, turn off the video, grab the vacuum cleaner, and perform a little damage control. If everyone is stressed, maybe it's time to cover the couch with a huge tarp or slipcover and conceal the clutter! Sometimes you just have to pick your battles.

Try to use a schedule, either a chore schedule or a planner. Write it down, keep it in your purse, and post it on the fridge or on a wipe-off board. As needs change and children grow, shuffle things around and give little ones more responsibility. I encourage you to delegate as much as you can and enlist help.

HOMEwork: How to You Waste Your Time?

Complete the worksheet below, "How Do You Waste Your Time?"

Read the list of **time wasters** in the left-hand column. Now rank them, based on a 1-10 scale (with 1 being the most and 10 being the least) in order.

Be honest while doing this exercise — take the time to do some soul-searching to see how you really spend your time.

How Do You Waste Your Time?

Time Waster	Ranking
Doing too much myself	
Clutter or Disorganization	
Running Errands	
Procrastination	
Meetings	
Telephone interruptions	
Putting out fires/resolving conflicts	
Unclear goals or priorities	

How Do You Waste Your Time?

Now based on the time management techniques
you've learned in this chapter (Chapter Three),
make an effort to change at least two of the items
on your list this month. Feel free to make notes to
yourself on this worksheet as a reminder to
change your priorities and eliminate distractions.

Refer to your worksheet in two weeks to monitor
your progress, and then follow up again at the
end of a one-month period. Did you reach your
goal? If so, congratulations! You're ready to tackle
two more time-wasters in the upcoming month.
Did you veer off course? Then it's time to slow
down and focus on eliminating at least one of the
chaos creators in your life next month. You can do
it!

 # Chapter Four: Purging Paper Clutter

Chaos or disarray of our papers can lead to financial clutter, and may even cause bad credit or bankruptcy. God encourages us to be good stewards in 1 Corinthians 4:1-2:

> *"Let a man regard us in this manner, as servants of Christ, and stewards of the mysteries of God. In this case, moreover, it is required of stewards that one be found trustworthy."*

What exactly is a steward anyway? Webster's II New Riverside Dictionary defines it as:

> *"One who manages another's financial affairs or property."*
> *"A person responsible for the household affairs of a large institution, as an estate."*
> *"A ship's officer responsible for provisions and dining arrangements."*

Are you up to the challenge of keeping your crew well fed and clothed by paying your bills routinely? Take time to read Jesus' words in Luke 16: 1-10, especially verses 10 and 11:

"Now He was also saying to the disciples, 'There was a certain rich man who had a steward, and this steward was reported to him as squandering his possessions.

And he called him and said to him, 'What is this I hear about you? Give an account of your stewardship, for you can no longer be steward.'

And the steward said to himself, 'What shall I do, since my master is taking the stewardship away from me? I am not strong enough to dig; I am ashamed to beg.

I know what I shall do, so that when I am removed from the stewardship, they will receive me into their homes.'

And he summoned each one of his master's debtors, and he began saying to the first, 'How much do you owe my master?'

And he said, 'A hundred measures of oil.' And he said to him, 'Take your bill, and sit down quickly and write fifty.'

Then he said to another, ' And how much do you owe? And he said, "A hundred measures of wheat.' He said to him, 'Take your bill, and write eighty.'

*And his master praised the unrighteous steward
because he had acted shrewdly; for the sons of
this age are more shrewd in relation to their
own kind than the sons of light.*

*And I say to you, make friends for yourselves by
means of the mammon of unrighteousness; that
when it fails, they may receive you into the
eternal dwellings.*

**He who is faithful in a very little thing is
faithful also in much; and he who is
unrighteous in a very little thing is
unrighteous also in much.**

**If therefore you have not been faithful in
the use of unrighteous mammon, who will
entrust the true riches to you?"**

We can't begin to pray for God's riches until we
can become trusted to take care of the little we are
given to budget and manage now.

Paper clutter is such a culprit, and can easily take
over our homes, filling every cabinet and drawer
to overflowing. There are a few simple techniques
that you can use to organize your system, then try
to keep it maintained on a regular (daily and
weekly) basis.

Use the *Four Steps of an Awesome Organizer* to set up
your system: Plan, Sort, Organize, and Maintain.

1. **Plan—** Jot down some notes to determine what you have, where it should go, what you need for storage, and how you will keep it up once established. Then start sorting!

2. **Sort —** This is the fun part, which you can easily do in front of the television or while listening to upbeat music. Label a few sturdy boxes or use the ones you created earlier in your organizing project, and then begin going through the paper piles, sorting into stacks as you go: To Pay, To File, To Follow Up, To Trash, Undecided.

HOMEwork – Paper Sorting 101

Use the labels provided in this study course to set up your sorting boxes for success:

- ❖ KEEP
- ❖ TRASH
- ❖ SELL
- ❖ UNDECIDED

Use double-sided tape, or rubber cement to adhere your signs to the boxes so that you can use them again and again.

Try to make a point not to read every single piece of paper you pick up. This otherwise easy stage of organizing can become a nightmare if you do! Do this all in one sitting if you have the luxury of having a large block of time, or just take 10-15 minutes a day until it's complete.

Since you're just sorting and categorizing by genre (catalog, bill, articles, essays, magazines) or action (needs paying, paid and should be filed, subscription to be archived for future research), it's easy to breeze through this once you get into the rhythm of sorting.

3. **Organize** — Now that you've recently purged your current papers, it's time to organize them so you don't have to keep repeating this dreadful step each month (or week, in some cases). Create two sets of files, **current** and **archived.**

HOMEwork - Plan for Success

Using the appropriate forms in this study course, plan your attack on the paper monster in your home. List items that will be stored in your **current files** and **archive files**, or if you trust your judgment, skip the writing step and move on. You can skip the writing, but don't skip the actual planning. This step allows you to stop and evaluate where your paperwork will actually be stored.

Another option is to purchase a professional file
system, such as FileSolutions©. I personally use
this in my own home and in the homes of my
clients, and can highly recommend it. The makers
of FileSolutions© have done all the indexing and
labeling for you. You only need to supply the
folders — they provide the rest. (Ordering
information is listed in the resource section in the
back of your study course.)

Current Files consist of things you access daily or
even weekly such as: bills to be paid,
appointments to be made, and anything else
requiring action (either today or in the near
future). Create simple categories for these items
with names that make sense to YOU and keep the
stacks separated in manila files or stacking bins. (I
recommend folders so that you can store them
vertically. Stacking bins are just one more place to
gather clutter!) Color-code if you think it will help
you stay focused, either by using colored folders
or colored dots on plain folders. Store in a
vertical stair-step rack on your desk or countertop,
or in hanging files in a small crate or desk drawer.
Just don't file these away so safely that you forget
where they are and stop using them!

PAPER MANAGEMENT FORM

Current Files		Archive Files	

Courtesy of Let's Get it Together, Copyright 2001

HOMEwork –It's all in the System

Take a break to gather together or purchase some file folders. You'll need:

- **Hanging Folders** – letter or legal sized, depending on your file holder. Get any colors you like. For special storage needs, invest in folders with a pocket for CDs or diskettes.
- **Folder Tabs** – I suggest clear plastic tabs so that you can easily read your labels. These usually come in the box with your hanging folders.
- **Manila Folders** – Five-cut in the color of your choice
- **A Fine-Tip Pen or Label Maker**
- **Folder Labels-** optional

Put these aside until you finish planning and sorting, then use them to organize your paperwork.

- *Archived Files* are those you've processed but need to retain such as: paid bills, receipts, warranties, tax records, business expenses, and so forth. Store them in your file cabinet inside hanging folders, and purge on a regular basis. Paid bills such as utilities and mortgages can be moved from your file cabinet to banker's boxes on a yearly basis to make room for the next year's paperwork. Be sure to label your boxes before storing so that you can find papers in a hurry for taxes or when selling a home.

Sort your paperwork as it arrives in your home, in categories such as To File, To Toss, To Pay, To Call, Follow Up Later, etc. Those become the titles or labels on your file folders, and make this whole process easier to deal with. Store your papers together in manila folders, pocketed folders, a binder with pocketed dividers, or an accordion file. The tool doesn't matter, but your system *does*. Perhaps you've used a system at work; don't hesitate to bring that concept home with you to make paperwork easier.

HOMEwork –Where Would you Put This?

Complete the worksheet **"Where Would You Put This Piece Of Paper?"** found on the next page.

Based on the four steps of organizing and the Paper Management 101 techniques, determine where you would put each piece of paper listed on the worksheet on the next page.

For instance, the first paper item on the list, *Kid's Christmas Craft Article*, might be filed in a manila folder labeled "To Read" until you can read the entire article. Or you may want to file it in your Arts & Crafts folder, or with Ideas. Depending on the priority, assign a home for the paperwork until you can take action.

Of course, if you've already read the article and want to keep it as inspiration for next year's Christmas crafts, then place it in the folder you have labeled for Christmas, Ideas, or Kids.

Notice there isn't a right or wrong answer here? Each person thinks differently,

WHERE WOULD YOU PUT THIS
PIECE OF PAPER?

Description of Paper	Where Would You Put It?
Kids Christmas Craft Article	
Unpaid Bill	
Automobile Inspection Receipt	
Permission Slip for a Field Trip	
Medical Explanation of Benefits	
Appointment Reminder from Your Dentist	
Your Child's Birth Certificate (original)	
End of Year Bank Statement for Taxes	
Other	

categorizing in her own unique way. Put it where YOU will find it — it's that easy!

Step 4: Maintain

As for those articles and the rest of the daily paper deluge, try to clip & toss as much as possible. Open mail over the wastebasket so that you can clip articles, and then file in a binder or photo album with magnetic sheets, or even a pocketed folder. Toss the remainder of the magazine or periodical to avoid clutter overload on your bookcase or magazine rack. Store the article in a folder labeled "To Be Read" until you have time to peruse, or once read, file in your cabinet for future reference. You'll find there's no need to keep the entire magazine or newsletter for one small article or recipe.

Parable of the Talents

Let's read Jesus' parable of the talents in Matthew 25:14-30:

> *"For it is just like a man about to go on a journey, who called his own slaves, and entrusted his possessions to them.*
>
> *And to one he gave five talents, to another, two, and to another, one, each according to his own ability; and he went on his journey.*
>
> *Immediately the one who had received the five talents went and traded with them, and gained five more talents.*
>
> *In the same manner the one who had received the two talents gained two more.*

But he who received the one talent went away and dug in the ground, and hid his master's money.

Now after a long time the master of those slaves came and settled accounts with them.

And the one who had received the five talents came up and brought five more talents, saying, 'Master, you entrusted five talents to me; see, I have gained five more talents.'

His master said to him, 'Well done, good and faithful slave; you were faithful with a few things, I will put you in charge of many things, enter into the joy of your master.'

The one also who had received the two talents came up and said, 'Master, you entrusted to me two talents; see, I have gained two more talents.'

His master said to him, 'Well done, good and faithful slave; you were faithful with a few things, I will put you in charge of many things; enter into the joy of your master.'

And the one also who had received the one talent came up and said, 'Master, I knew you to be a hard man, reaping where you did not sow, and gathering where you scattered no seed.

*And I was afraid, and went away and hid your
talent in the ground; see, you have what is
yours.'*

*But his master answered and said to him, 'You
wicked, lazy slave, you knew that I reap where I
did not sow, and gather where I scattered no
seed.*

*Then you ought to have put my money in the
bank, and on my arrival I would have received
my money back with interest.*

*Therefore take away the talent from him, and
give it to the one who has the ten talents.'*

*For to everyone who has shall more be given,
and he shall have an abundance; but from the
one who does not have, even what he does have
shall be taken away.*
*And cast out the worthless slave into the outer
darkness, in that place there shall be weeping
and gnashing of teeth.*

Are you ready to maintain the talents God has
entrusted to you as steward of *your*
household? Can you create order from chaos,
create a budget where there once was none,
and transform overspending into savings?

I think you can do it because you're not alone. Remember that you can do all things through Christ who strengthens you! (see Philippians 4:13).

Three STEPS TO KEEPING YOUR IN-BOX CLUTTER FREE

You can reduce paper clutter in your home or office by eliminating junk mail, faxes, and calls from solicitors. The following is contact information that will allow you to remove your name from junk mail, telemarketing, and junk fax lists:

JUNK MAIL:
Mail Preference Service
1120 Avenue of the Americas
New York, NY 10036-6700

Special Note: When placing phone orders with vendors, request that your name be kept confidential and not released to mailing lists.

TELEMARKETERS:
Telephone Preference Service
P.O. Box 1559
Carmel, NY 10512

JUNK EMAIL
E-Mail Preference Service
Register online at:
www.dmaconsumers.org/consumerfaqs.html

Closing Thoughts-

Congratulations! You've graduated from the
ranks of the organizationally challenged and
obtained the status of Awesome Organizer!
Whether it's the kitchen, car, or home office, you
can use the **four basic organizing principles** to
organize any area of your life. You're ready to go
forward and put your house in order. It's time to
conquer the clutter; to spend less time cleaning
and more time playing. Get ready to manage your
time and create more hours in your day for leisure
and fun. You've earned the right to live a
wonderfully organized, balanced life. Happy
organizing!

Debbie Williams
November 2002

How to Contact Us

I'd love to hear about your success stories, as well as your challenges. Whether you use one or many of the organizing principles contained in this study course, let me hear what works for you and your family, what doesn't work, and ways that you have modified some of the systems learned from reading the home management materials.

You can write to me at:

Debbie Williams
Let's Get It Together
P.O. Box 590860
Houston, TX 77259

Or send me an email:
Debbie@organizedtimes.com

Thanks for sharing!

Chapter Five: Organizing Tools

o **Websites** – useful places to shop and research
   online
o **Catalogs** – shop or plan from home by direct
   mail. Be sure to pick and choose your
   catalogues to avoid paper overload
o **Books** – even if you don't have time to read a
   book cover to cover, you'll enjoy perusing
   through the index or table of contents for quick
   reference in these recommended titles.
o **Products** – favorite organizing products for
   clutter control and scheduling

ONLINE ORGANIZING RESOURCES

Storage Solutions -

EZ Pocket
hanging pocket organizers for the week, month, or current projects
www.ezpocket.com

GetOrganizedInc.
Storage solutions for your home
www.getorginc.com

Lillian Vernon
organizing products for parents and teachers
www.lillianvernon.com

OfficeMax
supplies, furniture, and storage containers for home and office
www.officemax.com

What's On the Agenda -

Family Organizer
The planner that helps keep you organized
www.thefamilyorganizer.com

FranklinCovey
solutions for boosting personal and business
effectiveness
www.franklincovey.com

GoMom! Planner
A planner for busy mothers
www.Gomominc.com

Paper Management -

FileSolutions
Color-coded organizing systems for home,
students, and home office
www.file-solutions.com

Taming the Paper Tiger Software
Use your computer to solve your problems with
filing and managing paper
www.thepapertiger.com

Around the House-

OrganizedTimes
organizing solutions for your busy life
www.organizedtimes.com

Travel Aids-

Mobile Office Organizers
automotive office products
www.mobilegear.com

Education & Support –

ADHD of the Christian Kind
providing great hope in the Lord to deal
effectively with these differences
www.christianadhd.com

Messies Anonymous
support for messies online
www.messies.com

Living the Good Life

Home-Based Working Moms
(www.HBWM.com) is an online community and
professional association dedicated to helping
working moms stay closer to their children. In

addition, HBWM offers the unique Work-at-Home Kit (www.WorkAtHomeKit.com) for parents who are interested in working from home.

Be sure to sign up for a free subscription to their e-Newsletter:
mailto:hbwmoms-e-news-subscribe@yahoogroups.com

SheLovesGod - Get a Faith-Lift (www.shelovesgod.com)

CATALOGS

Home Decorators Collection – decorative accents and innovative solutions to organize your household clutter
800-245-2217
www.homedecorators.com

Ikea – great crates, baskets, and storage solutions
800 434-4532
www.ikea-usa.com (for US shoppers)

Lillian Vernon – home and home office products
800-545-5426
www.lillianvernon.com

Current USA – stationery and gifts
877-665-4458
www.currentcatalog.com

Office Max - home office and household
organizers
800-283-7674
www.officemax.com

Pick up a catalog from any of these fine retail
stores for at-home perusing, or visit their websites
for catalog and ordering information.

BOOKS

Home Management 101: A Guide for Busy
Parents, by Debbie Williams. Champion Press.
ISBN 1891400215

Creative Correction by Lisa Whelchel. Tyndale
House Pub. ISBN 1561799017.

Frozen Assets: How to Cook for a Day and Eat for
a Month by Deborah Taylor-Hough. Champion
Press Ltd. ISBN 1891400614.

Home Office Life by Lisa Kanarek. Rockport
Publishers. ISBN 1564967751.

How to Be Organized in Spite of Yourself: Time
and Space Management That Works With Your
Personal Style by Sunny Schlenger New American
Library. ISBN 0451164695.

How to Raise a Family and a Career Under One Roof: A Parent's Guide to Home Business by Lisa M. Roberts. Unknown. ISBN 0943641179.

Making a Home. Meredith Books. ISBN 69621203.

Organizing Your Home Office For Success: Expert Strategies That Can Work for You by Lisa A. Kanarek. Blakely Press. ISBN 0964347016.

Personality Plus for Parents by Florence Littauer. Baker Book House Co. ISBN 800757378.

Taming the Paper Tiger at Home by Barbara Hemphill. Kiplinger Books. ISBN 0938721577.

The Way They Learn by Cynthia Ulrich Tobias. Focus on the Family Pub. ISBN 1561794147.

RECOMMENDED PRODUCTS

File Solutions Organizing Systems for home, students, and home office. Each kit includes a FileSolutions® guidebook, FileIndex™, and pre-printed labels.
FileSolutions
PO Box 516381
Dallas TX 75251-6381
Phone: 972-488-0100
Email: fsservice@filesolutions.com
www.filesolutions.com

EZPocket Organizers
Keep weekday or project files close at hand for easy review and retrieval. Grommets make it easy to hang these organizers anywhere and free up valuable horizontal space.
EZ Pocket
1191 South Yosemite Way
Suite #47
Denver, CO 80231
Phone: 1-800-681-8681
Email: ezpocket@ezpocket.com
www.ezpocket.com

Mom Central
Think of Mom Central as everything a Mom knows filed and spiraled between two covers. A beautifully designed book filled with hundreds of lists that will help you organize your busy life with kids.
Mom Central
Mail Orders: 440 Beacon St. Chestnut Hill, MA 02467
Online Orders: www.momcentral.com or www.amazon.com

Post-it®Flags
A convenient, effective way to flag and index information, Post-it® Flags come in a variety of attention-grabbing colors, sizes and pre-printed messages. Choose an action-oriented pre-written flag or get creative and write your own.

3M Company
Available at Staples and Office Max stores
nationwide
Order online at: www.3m.com/Post-it
phone: 888-364-3577

Alternative Organizing Solutions —
Answer Key to Home Management 101
Exercise #1:

Wooden Cigar Box – decorative holder for all
those remote controls, message center near the
phone, arts and crafts box for your budding
Picasso

Film Canister – laundry money for your college
student, quarters for your car (tolls, parking
meters, vending machines), paper clips and
thumbtacks

Makeup Bag – portable office supply drawer for
your purse or briefcase, a comb and mirror for
your car, first aid kit for your car or van

Zippered Pencil Case – art supplies for the
backseat of your car, container for pens and
pencils in the junk drawer, portable office in your
home or van

3-Ring Notebook- fill with pocketed dividers for
a bill-paying organizer, greeting card organizer,
or project planner

Dishwashing Tub – cubby for kid toys on shelves or floor, store small tools nicely on garage shelving, creates a small sandbox for preschoolers when filled with cornstarch and measuring cups

Plastic Coat Hanger – belt/scarf/purse organizer for your closet, holds a mesh laundry bag on your bedroom door, makes a nice valet for hubby's sports coat

Plastic Milk Crate- smallest size makes a great kid console for the back of your car seat, square-shaped ones easily store hanging files for product literature or PTA papers, and larger ones contain clutter in transit (groceries, videos, library books, backpacks)

Wooden Peg Rack- towel rack for the bathroom, dress-up area for your child's room, a Tween Rack™ for closet, and a backpack/purse organizer for the mudroom

Canvas Book Bag- Grab-N-Go™ bag for outbound videos and library books, activity bag for small children during doctor's visits and restaurant waits, mail bag for your car so that important bills and documents don't slip through the cracks

Over-the-Door Shoe Bag – organize Beanie Babies®, corral household cleaners, contain junk drawer items in the home office

Trash

Keep

Sell

Undecided

Printed in the United States
812800001B

9 780972 698306